British & Australian

BBQ

SECRETS

BY
BENJAMIN BARTLETT &
ROSS YARRANTON

© Benjamin Bartlett & Ross Yarranton 2023

All rights reserved. No part of this publication may be reproduced, stored in a retrieval system or transmitted, in any form or by any means, electronic, mechanical, photocopying, recording or otherwise, without the authors' prior written permission.

Published in April 2023

A catalogue record for this book is available from the British Library

ISBN: 9798390938096

Imprint: Independently published

B Bartlett
Tel: +44 (0) 7941 222745

R Yarranton
Tel: +61 (0) 415 771172

Websites: www.bbqben.com & www.barbitec.com

Preface

Ben Bartlett & Ross Yarranton

Both Experienced Professional BBQ Chefs, one in the UK and one in Australia

Techniques can be different, but distance is no barrier, hence this first book.

Ben & Ross are both here to inspire great BBQ cooking!

'This book is not necessarily about recipes or techniques (although a lot revolves around that of course) it's more about passion and getting all your potential BBQ cooks and Chefs out there getting it right.

Believe us when we say that there are so many out there that burn, overcook, undercook, ruin and often kill a good BBQ mood and the food!'

This book is written with our joint passion and intended to make your own BBQ experience simple and enjoyable.

HAPPY

BBQ'ing!

Ben Bartlett

About the Authors:

Ben is a qualified UK BBQ Chef, world and UK BBQ Champion; Ross is an Australian BBQ Chef but his qualifications are more on the technical side, for this he can tell you what BBQ to buy and what BBQ is suitable for you, how it works, what heat cooks a good meal, what temp to cook at and whether a gas or charcoal BBQ is better for you. Also, whether plate or grill. Remember size does not matter, Ben & Ross can cook for 30 on a small two burner BBQ easily. It's just that timing and resting are so important to achieve a good result.

If you like a large BBQ in a lovely Alfresco area that's great and well-deserved, note that a big BBQ is only great if you know how to cook on it. Often people buy a big BBQ as the retailer has 'upsold' it to them and then it sits in the garden just waiting to be used…

Our authors love the 'BBQ beginner' so start small and then build to a bigger BBQ when you get more experienced if you think you need one.

Ben and Ross hope that you enjoy the benefits of their first joint book, "it's been great writing it and we hope that future BBQ Champions enjoy it. There will be another one coming when our new BBQ Gurus get a little more experienced, maybe in a year or two!"

Love to all you BBQ cooks out there!'

Ben & Ross

We are using a combination of British and Australian BBQ techniques, so although the recipes may seem easy, they may be a challenge to the novice BBQ user, to the seasoned one it contains those useful tips and simple recipes that can be built on to make you a BBQ 'natural'.

Contents

1. ABOUT BARBECUING 7
2. TYPES OF BBQ 9
3. TYPES OF COOKING 13
4. AUSTRALIAN BBQ 15
5. COCKTAILS 19
6. SPORT 22
7. BBQ COME RAIN OR SHINE 24
8. THE SAUCY SIDE OF THE GRILL 26
9. UNUSUAL FOOD COMBINATIONS 28
10. FISH 31
11. MEATS 35
12. BBQ 'LOW N SLOW' – FROM ROSS & BEN 41
13. USEFUL TIPS FROM BEN 43
14. USEFUL TIPS FROM ROSS 46
15. BBQ SAFETY 51
16. CLEANING UP! 53
17. RECIPES FROM BEN & ROSS 59
    GLOSSARY 110

About Barbecuing

Whilst general cooking maybe an art form, cooking on a BBQ can be simple and easy or complicated and hard. It really is easy to get wrong: overcooked, undercooked, burnt or rare. For the newest BBQ users, we want to make it:

'As easy to cook on a BBQ as it is to boil a kettle'.

There are a few things however to remember

A BBQ is an appliance that gets hot, whether gas or charcoal, so you really need to keep an eye on the temperature for safety's sake. Getting hot means that a BBQ can reach high temperatures. 250c and above is not uncommon, but there really is no need to let one get that hot. The highest that we get one too is about 200c, and occasionally over that to 220-230c is for an initial pork roast crackling. Kamado grills will get hotter, but that is for our next book; this book one is for the average BBQ and the new or more experienced cook.

In almost every case, cooking on a BBQ will cause fat build-up either on the grill or plate or in the drip tray. This is quite normal, but keeping the temperature to a maximum of 200c will ensure that the BBQ won't overheat and will be easy to control. All the recipes in our book will tell you what temperature to cook at and which burners go on either under the hotplate and/or under the grill. We'll go into the various types of BBQ in the next chapter, but for now, using the grill is what gives your food flavour as the fat and juices fall on to the 'flame tamer' or 'flavorisers' (the bit between the top plates/grills and the burners) and then flare up onto your food causing the charred look and BBQ flavour, again not burnt but charred.

There is nothing scary in BBQ cooking; just make sure that the temperature is controlled and the cooking surfaces have little to no fat on them. The oils go on the food first, NOT on the cooking surfaces, especially Extra Virgin Olive Oil. This oil has a low smoke point, so it will burn as soon as it hits the plate. Canola oil, Grapeseed oil etc., have high smoke points, so a little spray or brush with these oils is fine, as this keeps the surfaces lubricated to prevent sticking.

So, in recapping, no need to get your BBQ up to a high temperature unless a recipe specifically calls for it. A LOW and SLOW *cook* will save gas/charcoal, will be easier to clean up and will make your food more succulent to eat.

Types of BBQ

Over the years, the BBQ portfolio has changed a lot across the seas. In Australia, gas used to be the dominant cooking type, but charcoal now has a great return!

Smoking is also a 'new' thing, but that will be explained more in a later chapter.

In Australia, charcoal can be a difficult source of cooking as total fire bans prohibit their use; gas is therefore the easiest, most popular and most reliable cooking module.

OK, let's get down to the types of BBQ out there:

Manufacturers in Britain and Australia seem to have just found that making a BBQ that can do charcoal and gas cooking is cool. That's great to have such a versatile BBQ, and for a great price. However, this may not always be practical. So, most Barbecues out there fall into maybe 8 categories:

- The Flat Plate BBQ
- The Plate & Grill BBQ
- The Portable BBQ
- The Flame Failure BBQ
- The Indoor BBQ
- The 'Egg Type' BBQ
- The Marine BBQ
- The Infra-Red BBQ
- The Gas /Charcoal combo

We won't go into a total lowdown on these types, but maybe the most popular:

- The flat plate
- And, of course…
- The plate & grill
- And the Charcoal BBQ

British & Australian BBQ Secrets

THE FLAT PLATE BBQ

OK, this is the one with all plates, very popular at clubs and pubs as it's easy to clean and cheap to buy. Personally, I really wonder why people buy them as you may as well just cook in a frying pan as there really is no 'BBQ' flavour. However, they are available and fairly cheap, although more expensive ones are available too, both to run on LPG and Natural Gas.

THE PLATE AND GRILL

Now we are talking! The best BBQs around have plates and a grill. The plate to sear and cook eggs, and the grill to get that lovely BBQ flame and flavour. They range from very cheap to very expensive LPG gas or Natural Gas, charcoal, built-in or on a trolley; Gas ones have 1,2,3,4,5,6,8 burners, some with a side burner, wok burner, back burner, infra-red burners etc., wow that was a lot to take in… Let's try and break it down a bit…

Most barbecues now, apart from full plate BBQs (although some more expensive ones do), have a roasting hood. This makes it into an oven, and how versatile is that? You can cook bread, roasts, quiche, virtually anything on a BBQ now; there is one problem, though, temperature. Whereas a conventional oven has seals and fans to regulate the temperature, a hooded BBQ doesn't. To the skilled BBQ'er this is not a problem; to the novice, it can be. You might have tubular burners, cast iron, infra-red or just plain steel ones; they all do the same…cook your food!

Side or wok burners are great for stir-fries and fish and stuff that makes smoke or smell perfect for outside.

Just be careful in how you regulate the temperature; that will become more apparent in the recipes we have in this book, but the basics are to start low and build up, put on one or two burners, and, see the temperature on the hood and build the temperature up. Don't put them all on at once for a long time; there is no need, the food will burn, and your guests will not come back! Low and slow cooking is the way to go:

LOW & SLOW IS THE WAY TO GO – a temperature chart is in this book, so use it…

THE CHARCOAL BBQ

The all-time winner in BBQ cooking, the reason why charcoal BBQs have been the start of all BBQs is that the briquettes, charcoal, wood coals, whatever you want to call them, give off 'infra-red' heat, so they are a very efficient way of cooking. Infrared heat is what the sun has; that is, it only heats what it hits. Also, the advantage of a 'kettle' type BBQ for cooking a roast is that the initial heat of the fuel is hot, and after time, the heat gets lesser and lesser, so the initial heat sears your roast, and then it cooks slower.

Charcoal and Gas

A new innovation is to combine charcoal and gas; some BBQs and Pizza ovens have the option to use both forms of heat, so you get two for the price of one; although gas is a lot more convenient and cleaner, charcoal is there for that rustic woody flavour effect…

Choosing a BBQ?

It can sometimes be difficult to choose the right BBQ for your particular needs:

- How big?
- Grill or plate?
- Charcoal or Gas?
- Hooded or plate?

Yes, lots of questions before answers. Just think two things: How much and what do you want your BBQ to do?

Ross and Ben have spent a lot of hours cooking on a lot of barbecues, gas, charcoal, briquettes, wood etc., over the years. Not anyone is the better one; it just depends on you and on your own particular needs.

You can spend a lot of money on a BBQ and then not a lot. Don't get carried away by the salesperson at the store. All barbecues can do the same, grill, smoke, sear and cook.

Our advice is to start small and then, if needed, get a bigger one; remember that if you 'time and prep' well, you don't need an enormous BBQ (unless you want it just for show, that is!)

Just be careful what you buy and make sure it's within your own budget.

TYPES OF COOKING

There are 3 types of cooking on a BBQ:

SLOW

Slow cooking is for cuts like Brisket, Pulled Beef, Lamb, and Chicken etc., We aren't going to go through all those meats in this book, but once you have mastered one of them, the others follow.

Slow cooking means that **slow**. Cooking on a BBQ does not mean high heat for certain types of cooking. For example, to slow cook a roast, the hooded temperature might be about 150-160c for 3 – 4 hours, whereas a 'normal roast' would be about 200c for 1.5 hours.

INDIRECT

Moving on to indirect cooking, this is where the roast makes its entrance on a Gas BBQ, The Roast goes onto the plate, and the burners go on under the grill, hood down. That way, the heat moves through the grill up to the hood and over the roast, so the burners or source of heat is not on directly under it. Kettle BBQs will have the same system, but the coals will probably be on the sides with the roast in the middle, so the heat moves up over the roast.

The only time the gas burners may be on under the plate is when you initially start up the BBQ, but again that will be in the recipe.

DIRECT

Most BBQ cooking is done this way, chops, burgers, sausages, or Snags (Australian talk!) in other words, direct on the plate or grill with the burners on underneath it; this applies to any heat, whether gas or charcoal.

All 'full plate' BBQs will normally work this way as the burners are directly underneath it. Direct grilling works the same way, but this time there will be a 'Flame Tamer' or 'Vaporizer' which will allow

British & Australian BBQ Secrets

the juices of the meat to hit the 'tamer' before being caught on the burners and adding the BBQ flavour to the food. It also protects the burners from getting clogged up or flaring too much when cooking like this.

Charcoal and briquettes work slightly differently as the juices are allowed to fall on to them and spit back up to the food; hence they are really the vaporisers as well as the source of heat.

Australian BBQ

People joke about the Australians and their "Barbie", and the Australians do not really mind; they are passionate about them. The BBQ for an Australian is part of life and part of the culture and is not only a way of cooking food but also a gathering of people. In fact, it is fair to say that for some Aussies, a weekend is not a weekend without a Barbie.

Essential BBQ Herbs & Spices

The BBQ in Australia dates back to the days when the first white settlers arrived on the distant shores. It started firstly out of necessity and secondly because the weather is pretty much perfect for outdoor eating all year round. In the 1980s, Australians and their BBQs became noticed worldwide thanks to a superb advert with Paul Hogan, who invited people to visit and throw "a shrimp on the Barbie." Since then, Australians and their BBQs have gone hand in hand.

Like BBQing all over the world, the Australian Barbie has become more of an art form than it perhaps once was, but it doesn't stop traditionalists from doing their thing. A Barbie is as much a pastime as it is a way of cooking, and, just as in many countries, it is still very much a man's domain.

An Australian BBQ can be as simple or as cordon bleu as you like, but either way, in most cases, it is all about the company and less so the food. Many people would be happy with a good piece of meat, more than likely a good piece of Australian lamb eaten straight off the grill as a sandwich. Of course, there will be some snags; snags are not problems; they are sausages. For many locals, some meat, snags and a beer or Tinny will always make the perfect BBQ down under.

Australians are not afraid to cook a few things that are so very Australian. Lamb, beef, pork and chicken are as common or popular as they are anywhere else in the world. However, there are some meats you may not experience anywhere else other than Australia that are known to be cooked on the grill from time to time.

Do not be surprised to find you are offered kangaroo to eat. Roo meat, as the locals call it, is lean and has almost no fat. It cooks well and is extremely healthy. So, what if visitors from overseas roll their eyes and think of Skippy, Kangaroos run wild in Australia and thus make generous eating. Another meat you may get to try is Emu, a little like the South African Ostrich meat; having an Emu steak is a tremulously healthy option and tastes delicious.

As for the side dishes, in Australia, expect the usual array of salads and some fresh bread. All this is accompanied by some ice-cold Australian beer, and for those who don't like beer remember Australia has some of the finest wines in the world. Of course, there is always the option of sherry for your Sheila, but overall an Australian BBQ is a relaxed, casual affair that is meant to be enjoyed.

An Aussie BBQ is about people; it is about family, and don't be surprised to have neighbours drop in because, after all, everyone deserves good neighbours.

Cocktails

When it comes to a barbecue, most people expect a few cold tinnies and a few chilled glasses of wine to be served. One would be pushing the limits of the barbecue with a Gin and Tonic or Vodka and Orange. A Barbecue is for some reason, a beer and wine event, but it doesn't have to be.

A barbecue can be turned into a cocktail party with relative ease. It doesn't have to be a cocktail party where the ladies wear their smart frocks and men dress to the nines, but it could be. No matter what it will a barbecue your friends never forget. Who knows, you may even start a new trend in barbecuing?

The trick to having cocktails lies in the planning, as it does with any successful barbecue. Knowing what food will be on the menu determines what should be on the cocktail menu. As one might pair a good wine with certain foods, so one pairs a cocktail, or rather the ingredients of the cocktail. Having the right cocktail can make your barbecue the best barbecue ever by allowing flavours to mingle and merge with the smell of the grill.

What works with what?

When it comes to cooking rich meat such as lamb, beef or even pork, then cocktails made from darker, richer spirits match well. Cocktails mixed with good Scotch or Irish whisk(e)y, bourbons or the more modern aged tequilas work extremely well. Foods such as chicken cooked in rich marinade also go well with these types of cocktails; sometimes, bourbon can even be used in the marinade to give it a special lift.

When cooking lighter foods such as fish or vegetables, lighter, sweeter and fruitier cocktails become almost part of the food giving a real sense of summer to the barbecue. There is no hard and fast rule about what cocktail goes with what food, but having a cocktail that works with the food does make a difference.

ON THE DAY

Don't go overboard and try and make every cocktail you can imagine; this can mean the person cooking the food becomes a full-time bartender as well as a chef. Stick to a few simple cocktails that use similar ingredients; too many cocktails can turn a barbecue into an overcomplicated affair and making it memorable for the wrong reasons. Practice making the cocktails in advance; if you can perfect just one, two or maybe three cocktails, your guests be much happier.

Have plenty of ice and plenty of soft drinks to mix the cocktails with; on a hot summer day, you want to keep your guests hydrated, not make them totally tipsy in the first 15 minutes. With the ice and the soft drinks, a proper cocktail shaker along with measuring glasses, or ideally, put bottles on an optic to get accurate measures, will ensure your cocktails are made as they should be. The making and shaking can become part of the fun.

Secret Note: A cocktail party is a great way to restock your drinks cabinet. Tell each of your friends to bring the ingredients for their cocktail, and because there is no way they can truly use up all the spirits, they get left behind. This works like a charm!

SERVING THE COCKTAILS

Just as you would serve the food from your barbecue in a manner befitting the food, your cocktails should be served in the same way. Part of the pleasure of a cocktail BBQ is in the creativity. Cocktails served in boring glasses without the fancy straws, fruit and umbrellas look boring, and that makes your BBQ boring. Invest in a few coloured straws and some umbrellas and skewer some fresh summer fruit onto cocktail sticks, and even if you haven't quite mastered flaring, your drinks are at least fun. Give the names of the cocktails if they are something you have made up; it can also be fun.

Remember to drink responsibly and don't drink and drive. We are off now to enjoy a barbecue blinder… my own secret barbecue white sangria cocktail with grilled fruit!

TOP TIP

The best Gin and Tonic is made with charred lemon. Slice a lemon in half and chargrill for a few minutes on a hot grill.

Sport

Australians turn rugby matches into an excuse to light the fire. "Put another shrimp on the Barbie, mate" is a common joke about Australians. South Australians love their lamb chops, Victorians their beer, and Queenslanders their steak, with West Australians split between beer and steak. Many will have the onions and snags (sausages) sizzling. Americans turn match day into a barbecue too, and it indicates that sport and a BBQ go together like a perfectly cooked steak and an ice-cold beer.

Anyone who takes their sport and their BBQ seriously will tell you that the weather doesn't play a part in making the day work. Football is a winter sport, and that means the weather may not play along, and careful planning will ensure the success of the BBQ no matter what. Other sports take place all year round, and watching sports at home with a BBQ creates an atmosphere that makes the match, tournament or overall event something special.

Planning is vital when it comes to having a BBQ around a sporting event. Knowing when a match kicks off or ends are important. Cooking all the food and missing the match or event defeats the object. Knowing the times means food can be cooked before and eaten during, cooked quickly at half-time, or cooked after the event.

When having a BBQ with a sports event, keep things simple yet tasty. Fast-cooking foods or finger foods are a great idea. A simple selection of kebabs made with chicken, peppers and onions cooked on skewers makes a tasty and filling dish to cook on the BBQ. Kebabs cook quickly and can even be cooked at half-time in some cases.

Homemade burgers are perfect for a sports event BBQ, but add some fun and tell people they must make their own patties. Supply a variety of toppings, and people can munch during the match; burgers can also be kept warm and can be pre-cooked before an event and then warmed on the BBQ before eating.

Wimbledon is a great excuse for a sporty BBQ. Tell your guests to wear tennis outfits and have a BBQ with strawberries, cream, and some quintessential Pimm's. A lunchtime BBQ before the men's final can be a superb way to ooh and aah your way through a game of tennis.

A sporting event is a wonderful excuse to invite friends and family around, set up the living room so everyone can see the game or move the TV nearer the BBQ to create the atmosphere. Then it is ready… steady… BBQ!

Make every sports event a BBQ and win or lose; everyone is happy!

BBQ Come Rain or Shine

When someone hears the word "Barbecue," they think of shorts, t-shirts, sunshine, and blue skies. A BBQ is considered a summer activity, something that is only done a few times a year. However, all those people who only light the fire or turn on the gas in the summer months are missing out; a BBQ can happen come rain or shine, even during winter or a wet late autumn afternoon.

The secret to a BBQ outside of summer is to do so under cover and ideally stay dry; hence investing in a waterproof gazebo will be one of the best investments you ever make. If you don't have a gazebo, your second best is a good friend with a big umbrella; this can be great fun.

But seriously, your BBQ should not go under wraps for another ten months just because the weather turns colder and the rain starts to pour down. Come on; the UK is hardly famous for its long tropical summers. Far too many Barbecue parties are cancelled because the weather is a little more inclement than hoped for, and this should not be so; all over the world, people light up their barbecues in all kinds of weather, and you can too.

A winter or unseasonal BBQ can be fun and warm food on a wet, blustery, or even snowy day really does taste amazing. For the chef, the BBQ becomes his or her source of warmth in the cold; a little secret is to use two barbecues or one barbecue and something in which to make a fire. Using one fire to cook on and the other to stay warm really does work well, and a warm glass of Mulled White Wine Sangria (see recipes) goes down extremely well!

Secondly, if you intend to make BBQing a year-round thing, why not build an awning or alcove undercover for your BBQ? In Australia, this is common; not only does it make a shelter from the weather, both pouring rain and blasting sunshine, but it makes the BBQ a feature that cries out to be used more often. Turning your BBQ into a feature of your home will, for some strange reason, win you quite a few friends and make any BBQ at any time of year something special.

Once you have sorted out how to stay warm and dry and out of the wind, it is time to cook up a storm and enjoy a wonderful winter meal. A mix of things that cook slowly and quickly is the ideal way to produce the perfect winter meal on a BBQ and can make a wonderful alternative to a traditional Sunday roast.

A slow-roasted joint of lamb, whole leg or a nice sized shoulder, ideally still on the bone, tastes magnificent when cooked slowly on the coals, or better still, some wood, but gas is equally fine. Prepare the meat the night before by marinating it overnight before wrapping it in foil and placing it on medium coals or heat for 3 to 4 hours. This is a real place-on-the-fire-and-leave dish, best cooked in a kettle or closed BBQ or with some turning, can be easily cooked on an open BBQ.

Wrapped veggies and other dishes are superb in winter; they don't need constant turning and supervision, so you can head indoors and warm up from time to time. A winter BBQ needs just a little bit of thinking, and wrapping veg and other items is just one tip that makes things easier and gives a chance to get creative.

Have you ever considered wrapping carrots or whole sweetcorn in bacon? Try it. Simply wrap each carrot or sweetcorn in some streaky bacon, place a handful on some foil, add some butter, wrap and place on your BBQ. BBQing in winter is simple when you know how.

Squashes, pumpkins and butternut are perfect for a winter BBQ. Sliced in two, wrapped in foil with a little butter and roasted on the fire. Again, these are very much placed on the coals and walk away, and that is part of the secret to a winter BBQ or even in summer when the weather turns a little unseasonal.

Don't be afraid to cook on your BBQ when the sun is not shining. Your BBQ can deliver amazing warm-you-up food that tastes wonderful and, wink wink, is not difficult to cook come rain or shine… some say the best-barbecued food is cooked when others give up and go inside.

The Saucy Side of the Grill

Q: What do a barbecue and a carry-on movie have in common?

A: THEY BOTH HAVE THEIR FAIR SHARE OF SAUCY MOMENTS.

Sauces at a barbecue are almost as important as the meat and the people. The sauces, like the meat and the people, can make or break your barbecue. Many barbecues stick to the usual tomato sauce and mustard, and some people venture further with sweet chilli or Tabasco, but there is so much you can do with a good sauce at your BBQ.

Whether the sauce is used to baste the food, pour over or is just there to dip things into, a good sauce will have your guests salivating and believing you are the king of all cooks. Sauces are generally simple, and very often, you can experiment before making a large batch, and there is never any fear of getting too creative. Some of the best sauces at barbecues I have attended have been the result of experimentation or accidents.

However, a good sauce should be well mixed; if it is too runny, you may as well pour your beer or wine on the food, and if it is too stodgy, you may as well replace the meat with the "sauce". The consistency is logical, but very often, knowing what flavours go with what is not so logical. Mustards make a great base for a sauce, and the type of mustard used can bring a host of flavours to the food from the grill. Dijon mustard is not as hot as English mustard, and adding a few ingredients such as vinegar, peach jam, some butter, and garlic gives a sauce with a difference. Keep in mind that you may be feeding kids and that some people don't like hot, spicy food. If you are making something spicy with some chillies, make sure you let people know.

Don't let your sauces take over the barbecue; the flavour of the food should be enhanced, not smothered. Lamb chops should allow the lamb flavour to flow; a sweet sauce or something with a hint of coriander can really go well with lamb.

To add a little sizzle to your burgers, mix a splash of Worcester sauce. For the adults, consider adding some bourbon into the ketchup. The old favourite of mixing mustard with ketchup is still something kids love. But there is nothing to stop you from making sauces from scratch with herbs, spices, olive oil and other ingredients. Homemade sauces and dips can boost your barbecue from bangers and burgers to something really special. A blender can become a good friend when making sauces, allowing for ingredients to be liquidised into the sauce. Adding apples to the sauce can sweeten it, for example.

Try something Asian using honey, sesame, and soy sauce. A sweet dipping sauce is perfect for dipping slithers of steak into and brings the Far East to your grill. Try it; you will need the following:

50mls honey, 1 teaspoon sesame oil, 1 teaspoon rice wine vinegar and 50mls soy sauce.

Put the ingredients into a bowl and whisk until combined. It is simple to make, and giving each person a small bowl of sauce to dip his or her steak into makes your barbecue posh and extremely tasty.

Have some fun with sauces. Don't be afraid to experiment because barbecuing is as much fun as it is food.

Unusual Food Combinations

A BBQ can become boring, and bangers and burgers can be a little lame, so why not spice things up with some unusual food combinations or foods from around the world?

Unboring Burgers

Burgers can be lame on the barbecue, but there is a weird food combination that gives the humble burger a completely new lease of life. Burgers with peanut butter work extremely well, taking this conventional BBQ food to a whole new dimension.

Toasted Sandwiches

In South Africa, a BBQ, or braai, is often accompanied by "Braaibroodjie" or toasted sandwiches. Traditionally these are cheese and tomato or even just tomato, but even in this world, food can be spruced up with an unusual food combo. Banana and cheese (Camembert really works well) is an excellent combination in a toasted sandwich that works surprisingly well, making a quick and easy starter while your guests await the main course.

Sweet Hot dogs

Just like the unboring burgers, the traditional hot dog can be given an unlikely twist. Most people serve mustard or ketchup with a hot dog but replacing these by smothering the bread roll with strawberry jam does something that sounds crazy but is wonderful…. and then crunch some Doritos on top!

Tequila and Chicken

Maybe save this for the adults. Who would ever imagine that Tequila would make a great marinade? It does, but it needs a little help from some freshly squeezed lime and orange juice. Mix up 120ml of gold Tequila (must be gold), 120 ml of fresh orange juice and 250ml of fresh lime juice. Pour over some chicken breasts and keep in the fridge overnight. Ask your guests what they think they were marinated in, and they will never guess the secret ingredient, but for some, it will be on the tip of their tongue!

Roosterkoek Bread

Ok, so it is a South African recipe but one that will become the most in-demand food at any barbecue you ever host. Bread and rolls can be boring, you can try all you like to try to get smart and buy fancy bread from a bakery, but you will never get better than this.

These are a breeze to make and take your BBQ back to the absolute basics when man first cooked on an open flame – boy scouts even make these on sticks. You will need 400g plain flour, a packet of dried yeast, a teaspoon of salt, 2 teaspoons caster sugar, 50 ml oil and about 250 ml water. Mix the yeast and sugar with about 100ml of water and let it foam. Mix the other ingredients in another bowl and add your yeast water. Knead for 5 minutes and then leave in a covered and oiled bowl to rise for an hour. Divide into 12 flattened balls and then leave to rise for 15 more minutes. Place on the fire and turn it a few times, and you will know when it is cooked. Easy and deliciously basic.

Pomegranate Meat

This weird and wonderful combination works well with any meat. Used as a marinade or thrown over when in the meat dish, people will wonder what on earth you are doing, and their faces will tell you what they are thinking. This is weird, but boy, does it work!

Banana Wrapped Bacon

I think this is one from the Aussies, as only they could attempt to fry bananas and succeed. Take a banana, wrap it in bacon, and throw it on the BBQ. Turn it gently and keep it on long enough just to crisp the bacon all around, then serve. Oh yes, serve by drizzling some honey over it… weird, tasty, and different.

These are just a few ways to spruce up your BBQ… come on, get creative because anything goes when it comes to a BBQ.

Fish

Many people will shy away from cooking fish on the BBQ, and seafood and BBQ are two words that do not seem to go together, but in fact, seafood and BBQ are great together, and if anything, seafood on the BBQ is easier than meat.

British & Australian BBQ Secrets

When it comes to Seafish, there are generally two types of fish you can throw on your barbecue: Filleted and whole. There is nothing to be afraid of when cooking fish, provided you get to grips with a few top tips. Once you have mastered fish on your BBQ once you will never fail again, and healthy and nutritious sustainable fish on your BBQ will become a family favourite.

Tip #1

KEEP THE SKIN ON

Yes, many recipes tell you to remove the skin and big fillets are generally prepared skinless. Because cooking fish on the BBQ requires some movement of food to ensure proper cooking, the skin holds it all together. Some fish, such as mackerel, have a skin that cooks well and forms a crispy and very tasty layer of food, but others have tough skin that becomes chewy and inedible. Either way, the skin can be removed with ease once cooked.

Tip #2

CHEAT: USE A FISH BASKET

No, this is not the wicker or straw basket pubs use to serve food in but rather a metal "clamp" that holds the whole or filleted fish in place to allow you to turn the fish. There are a variety of shapes and sizes. Extra Tip: Layer some fresh herbs inside the basket and add some flavour to the fish while cooking.

Tip #3

STEAM THE FISH

Steaming a fish is a superb way to cook fish on your barbecue. Take some tinfoil; grease the foil or use a spray to make it non-stick; place the fish, whole or filleted, in a tinfoil parcel along with some lemon slices and herbs; wrap the parcel tight, leaving a little room at the end for steam to escape. This technique only takes a few minutes for the fish to cook a few inches from the coals. Serve unwrapped and let your guests gently open the package and let the smell of fresh fish and lemons whet their appetite. Extra Tip: Making the parcel non-stick with butter or olive oil adds flavour to the fish

Tip #4

WOOD SHEETS

Wood sheets or papers can be used and come in a range of flavours, including oak, apple, maple, cedar, and mesquite. Soak the sheets first in apple juice, water or whisky for thirty minutes. Then place a fillet onto the sheet and cook on low-medium heat until the fish is cooked and the wood sheet is charred. This keeps the fish moist, and the wood gives it a lovely smokiness.

Tip #5

TWO SPATULAS

Flipping the fish is the part of cooking Seafish on the BBQ that scares people. The fear is that the fish will crumble when flipped. The trick to avoiding fish break up is to use two spatulas and place one on top of the fish as you flip the fish with the other underneath. A little oil brushed on the fish before grilling also makes the fish easier to flip, as it is less likely to stick. Extra Tip: An elegant way to cook Seafish and to stop it from sticking is to layer some sliced lemons on the grid and cook the fish on the lemons – tasty and totally non-stick.

Tip #6

CLEAN THE GRID

Fish has its own delicate flavour that can be easily spoilt, and any residue left on your grid from your last BBQ does this easily. Get your grid hot and give it a good scrub down with a wire brush. A clean grill will also be less likely to stick, and if need be you can brush it with some olive oil before putting your fish on the fire.

Cooking Seafish on the BBQ is easy when you follow these simple steps. On top of these tips, always ask your fishmonger for sustainable fish or fillets that are good for throwing on the BBQ; ask for larger cuts and, of course, the freshest fish.

Meats

The mainstay of any barbecue is beautifully prepared meat, but nowadays, your choice of farmed meat isn't limited to lamb, beef or pork. Many butchers across the UK and Australia now stock unusual meats from sustainable sources, so why not try ostrich, kangaroo or crocodile for your next barbecue? If you can't find these exotic delicacies, don't despair because a little help from the contents of your herb and spice rack can turn ordinary lamb, beef and pork into something truly extraordinary.

Searing any cut of beef, lamb, or pork couldn't be easier. For charcoal grills, place the meat in the centre of the cooking area; for gas grills, turn up the gas to high and leave the food for one minute before turning. Leave for a further minute, then turn the gas down, or move the food to a cooler part of a charcoal grill for the rest of the cooking time.

Marinades

Searing works best with good cuts of meat, but marinades will work with anything. In fact, I'd go so far as to say that marinades are the most important weapon in the war to convince people that barbecuing is the best form of cooking ever invented!

A good marinade not only flavours food but it also helps keep it moist and tender during cooking. At its most basic level, a marinade is just a mixture of herbs and spices held together by a binding agent, and most fall into one of two categories:

- Acidic marinades, based on wine, vinegar, mustard, soy sauce or citrus fruit juices that help tenderise the meat.
- Oil and paste marinades, which form a crust whilst cooking to seal in the juices that help tenderise the meat.

Of course, the secret is finding the right blend of herbs and spices to complement the food being cooked, and there are plenty of suggestions in the recipe section later in this book. Marinating for the correct length of time is crucial to bringing out the distinct flavours of different foods, but these times vary according to the size and type of food you want to flavour. As a general rule, you should allow 250ml of marinade for every 1lb of meat and marinate for the following times:

Food	Approximate marinating times
Fish	1 to 2 hours
Shellfish	30 minutes to 1 hour
Chicken (whole)	4 to 6 hours
Chicken (pieces)	2 to 6 hours
Turkey (whole)	Overnight (inside the fridge)
Turkey (pieces)	4 to 8 hours
Pork	3 to 4 hours
Red meat	Overnight (inside the fridge)
Kebabs	4 to 6 hours
Spare ribs	6 to 8 hours
Vegetables	60 minutes to 2½ hours

Rubs

A barbecue rub is simply a mix of ground herbs and spices rubbed into meat to enhance its flavour, but the vital extra ingredient that turns simple seasoning into a rub is sugar. During cooking, the sugar caramelises, forming a crust that seals in the juices and creates the sweet flavours that are so characteristic of American-style barbecued food.

As with marinades, rubs can be used wet (mixed with a binding agent into a paste) or dry (as a powder), but the crucial difference is that rubs are applied immediately before cooking. This makes rubs quicker and easier to use than marinades, and they're especially useful for campfires and other barbecues where long hours of marinating in huge vats of liquid are impossible.

That said, it's a good idea to let the meat rest for as long as you can after applying the rub so that the herbs and spices have a chance to penetrate. If you have the time, the marinating chart can also be applied to rubs.

To apply the rub, sprinkle the powder or spread the paste over the food smoothly and evenly. Use your fingertips or the back of a tablespoon to massage the herbs and spices into the meat gently. With dry rubs, a light brushing of olive oil or mustard will help the powder stick.

British & Australian BBQ Secrets

Sauces and glazes

Technically a sauce should only be applied after cooking has finished, but as some people like to brush food with a little zingy barbecue sauce whilst it's cooking to create a glaze, we'll give it a mention here.

A glaze is different to a rub or a marinade because it only flavours the surface of the meat rather than being absorbed throughout. Again, it's a quick and easy flavour enhancer.

To create a glaze, brush the sauce onto the food towards the end of the cooking process. Don't apply too early, or it'll burn; equally, don't leave it too late, or there won't be enough time for the sugar to caramelise. To recreate the high gloss shine that's such a distinctive feature of Chinese barbecued spare ribs, stir some honey into the sauce before brushing it on.

Steak

Cooking steak, the best and easiest way by Ross…

This is on a BBQ with a grill and plate, but you can use just a grill as the same method applies

Scotch Fillet Steak We all know how to cook a steak, don't we? Well, we should by now…I have a simple foolproof method to cook a steak that rarely fails, and it goes like this.

Scotch fillet is ideal for cooking on the barbeque for several reasons. It Comes with lovely marbled fat in the meat, which dissolves when cooked, Making the meat moist and tender. Also, it doesn't take long to cook, and tastes fantastic!

Heat the hotplate and grills on high for 10–15 minutes and when the hotplate and grills are hot enough, rub or spray some oil onto them (if they're not already oiled).

When the hotplate starts to smoke, place the oil-brushed steaks onto it and cook for 45 seconds only, then transfer to the grill the same side up (this is to get that ribbed look!). After about 2–3 minutes, the juices will start to come through to the top.

When this happens, turn the steak over and onto the hotplate again for 30 seconds, then back to the grill the same side up. It will take less time to Cook the other side. If you want it rare, cook the second side for about 2 minutes and for well-done, cook for about 4 minutes.

Let the steak rest for 4–5 minutes before serving. This will allow the meat to relax and allow the juices to flow, making it sumptuous and tender.

BBQ 'Low n Slow' – from Ross & Ben

You have probably heard from many BBQ cookbooks and cooking shows that if you cook 'slow and low,' you will have succulent meat for a 'budget cut'…

Ben & I have been advocates of this method of cooking long before the so-called experts.

Well, what exactly does this mean? Ben and I both have cooked 'low and slow', but has anyone explained how this can work in your favour on a BBQ? Yes, I know that we can put it into a recipe, and yes, I know that we have a chart that gives you an idea of what it means, but how do you do it?

Well…think of a BBQ like a 'Slow cooker'; most of you reading this will have one or have used an electric slow cooker. Think of a gas BBQ as a slow gas cooker and a charcoal BBQ as a slow charcoal BBQ.

Remember, both charcoal and gas can work the same way, but it means less gas and less charcoal. Let us explain….

GAS & CHARCOAL: the best way with gas and charcoal with a hooded BBQ is not to let the temperature go above 150c on the hood stat; this means keeping the burners on low and experimenting or adjusting them so that the temperature stays about 150c. This can be hard to monitor, and if it goes a little above, don't panic but do not let it get to 200c. Remember, a Gas BBQ has fiercer heat than a domestic oven, and the hood stat is not a true temperature indicator!

This might mean putting one or two burners on low and putting your roast on the plate or grill (preferably in a baking dish) on the opposite side to the lit burners. If all is a grill, as long as it is not under direct heat, this will still work, still getting that wonderful BBQ flavour.

In the case of charcoal, use less charcoal and put the roast away from the direct heat, i.e., if the coals are at each side, the baking tray goes in the middle, in other words, <u>NOT</u> directly under the coals and the lid on top, but you must keep an eye on the temperature. Once you have mastered this and have the right controlled temperature, you will have succulent food, and all your friends will want the technique!

You can slow-cook chicken, beef, lamb, pork or any protein this way; it just takes a bit of practice, so try it and let us know how you get on. The good thing about Barbecuing is that it's not an exact science. It takes a bit of skill and trial an error, but this book will take you through it and make you a great BBQ cook!

Useful Tips from Ben

A good BBQ is remembered for good food and great company. A great BBQ is one that not only has great company but superbly great food. BBQing to some is like magic; it looks like hard work looking on but, the audience is bluffed into believing just how masterful the chef is by simple tricks.

The Great BBQ Bluff is easy to achieve. While not all the BBQ secrets will ever be told, there are a few tips and tricks that make your audience believe you are the master of the BBQ. The first thing to remember is that there is no such thing as cheating when it comes to a BBQ, that is unless you have had someone BBQ you the food and all you are doing is warming it. The art of a BBQ is making the simple things look complicated by making them taste and smell divine.

Tip #1 – The Grill

Most BBQ'ers pet hate is food sticking to the grill or the grid. To BBQ #LikeABoss there are two secrets to non-stick food. The first is to clean the grid. Clean it when it is hot and do so with half an onion. Wire brushes work ok to get the heavy gunk off, but an onion does the business of cleaning. Then stop the stick. Brushing oil on the grid makes the grid slippery if you are cooking different courses or have a conveyor belt of food to cook brush between food sessions.

Tip #2 – The Coals

Using gas is a breeze, but to look the part and dazzle your guests cooking on coals is a must. It is not difficult when you know how, and you can even use the coals to turn up your bluff. Coals should not be flaming when you place the food on the grid. The perfect heat comes when the ashes are white. The trick is to use a little more charcoal or, if you are really showing off the wood. Let the coals pile up. To add to the cheat, light a mini-fire or BBQ chimney beside the main fire to allow coals to be shovelled, and you will never run out of heat.

British & Australian BBQ Secrets

The tip within tip #2 is throwing some herbs into the fire when cooking and creating smoke that flavours the food.

Tip #3 – The 24-hour marinade

Any chef or butcher will tell you that meat soaked in a marinade overnight or longer is the best. Brushing a marinade on at the time of cooking does little more than create something to burn and go black. Soaking chops or other cuts overnight in the fridge tenderises the meat and gives it an amazing flavour. Chicken breasts on the bone can be a pain, so pierce them with a fork, then soak them overnight in a little lemon juice or marinade and let the flavour soak in. This simple cheat will have your guests believing you are a marvel with a BBQ and a whizz in the kitchen!

Tip #4 – The Foil Oven

This bluff is the secret to cooking larger quantities of food without it going cold before serving. There are two types here, and both allow you to bluff your way to perfection. The first is to keep your meat warm and moist before serving. Take two aluminium foil containers and place one on top of the other; place the containers on the edge of the grill or fire and keep the food warm. The second is the ultimate way to cook veggies on the BBQ. From heavyweight foil, make a foil envelope, coarsely chop some veggies, add a little oil and place on the grill.

Bonus Tip: to boost your veggie dish on the grill, take an aluminium foil container and throw in the now-cooked veggies. Then mix a small tub of fresh cream with some vegetable stock together, throw over the veggies, stir, cover with foil and leave to bubble through. Your guests will be amazed at the magnificent and luxurious veggies.

Tip #5 – The secret to salmon or trout

Fish is often a clear steer item on a BBQ for obvious reasons. It sticks! There is a simple bluff to getting this perfect every time, and it involves lifting the fish off the grid. Layer the grid with slices of lemon and place the fish on them. Brush the fish with lemon juice. It will never stick, and then the secret is to turn the fish as little as possible.

Tip #6 – Let the meat sit.

Far too often, meat heads from the fire to the plate to be eaten. Every chef knows that all meat needs to rest, and the same is true with your BBQ. Just letting the meat sit for a few minutes will allow all the flavour to flood the meat, and it will taste perfect. A little time leads to perfection. #WorthTheWait

Tip #7 – Simple sweetness

Showing off your BBQ skills is easy, and with some simple dishes, you can cook dessert on the BBQ. A banana stuffed with marshmallows looks sophisticated and tasty, and it is. It is surprisingly simple, as bananas and marshmallows both cook very fast. This is a great one to convince kids that you are the BBQ King!

Tip #8 – Secret marinade for lamb

This is perhaps the cheekiest bluff of them all. Cola has a unique taste, and if you want to blow your guests away, soak a few lamb chops in some for a few hours. The stickiness and the flavour work wonderfully together, and the whole world will want to know the secret to your secret marinade.

Tip #9 – Apple Juice

This is Ben's favourite tip. Fill a new plastic garden hand sprayer with ordinary unsweetened apple juice and use it on any meat, beef, lamb, pork, chicken or fish, and it will help keep the meat moist and give it a lovely caramelisation.

These are just a handful of bluffs of hacks. There are countless others, but if I told you, I would have to do something very unpleasant, and that is just not good. A BBQ should be fun, the food should taste great, and none of it should be hard work. If you, even as the chef, are not enjoying the BBQ, then it is not a BBQ.

Summer is only around the corner; share your bluffs, tips, and tricks with us, and who knows, we may just try them ourselves.

Useful Tips from Ross

Meat thermometers, analogue and electronic

Using a meat thermometer to check on your meat has been around for a long time; recently, these probes have gone electronic and remote so that they beep you when your meat is rare, medium or well done. A great way to check, but it has some disadvantages.

You basically allow a prong to check, whereas the good old eye and prod will work better; it means you keep an eye on it, and you will gain experience in knowing when it's ready.

Most of these thermometers allow the food to be overcooked as; obviously, they want to make sure the food is cooked well. This means that if the probe goes to rare, it's close to a medium cook. Medium close to well done and well done overcooked! So, we would recommend the probe be used just to confirm your own view.

Having a BBQ means keeping an eye on the cooking and regular checking, as leaving it for a long time can mean the food is over-cooked, so every 15 minutes or so, check your roast to see if it's cooking ok and if you need to adjust the burners up or down, off or on. Again, cooking slowly gives you time to adjust the settings if you need to.

Remember, the art of a good BBQ cook and the fun of cooking is knowing when your food is ready and experimenting with the temperature and time; once you have this in hand, you will only need a thermostat to check it's cooked before resting. Knowing how your BBQ cooks will get you more than halfway to a success-ful BBQ.

Weather

Is it a hot day or cold? Is it raining, windy or fine? Almost always, the weather will affect your timings. If it's cold, obviously, your BBQ will take longer to heat up and cook; if it's warm and hot, it takes less time. Humidity too will make a huge difference, making a shorter journey for a roast to cook and keeping the moisture in.

For the Aussies out there, remember when there is a total fire ban, it means no open flamed Barbecues, like charcoal or briquettes or wood pizza ovens; the fines are very high, and as our climate is mostly dry, one spark can cause a huge fire…..

For the Brits, please remember, if you do have a BBQ outside your home, on the beach or in a park, please clear up after yourself and don't litter your beach.

Covers

Covering your BBQ will give it longevity and keep it looking nice, be careful, though; most of them don't have vents, and the BBQ can sweat and rust without proper ventilation. This happens mostly when it's outside not undercover, and it's been raining. Then the sun comes out, and the moisture on the ground rises up under the BBQ and having nowhere to go, it sits there and, after a while, will rust the BBQ; all you must do is take it off now and then to check, if there is moisture there leave it off for a while until it dries out.

Cooking with Gas, NG & LPG

There are two types of gas used in Barbecuing, Natural Gas (NG) and Propane / Butane LPG. Both are fairly common in Australia, NG, when the BBQ is in a built-in area or on a trolley with a NG bayonet connection to the house. In Britain, butane is mainly used; Patio Gas is one that has a mix of butane and propane; Natural Gas is not as common.

The difference between the gasses is that LPG is hotter and has a bigger pressure and NG is not as hot and has a lower pressure. NG vapour floats, and LPG vapour sinks. LPG comes from a gas cylinder, whereas NG comes from the house. Different rules apply in Australia if the BBQ is on Natural Gas than one on a bottle (LPG) also, propane is mainly used for Gas Barbecues there.

Cooking Temperature Graph

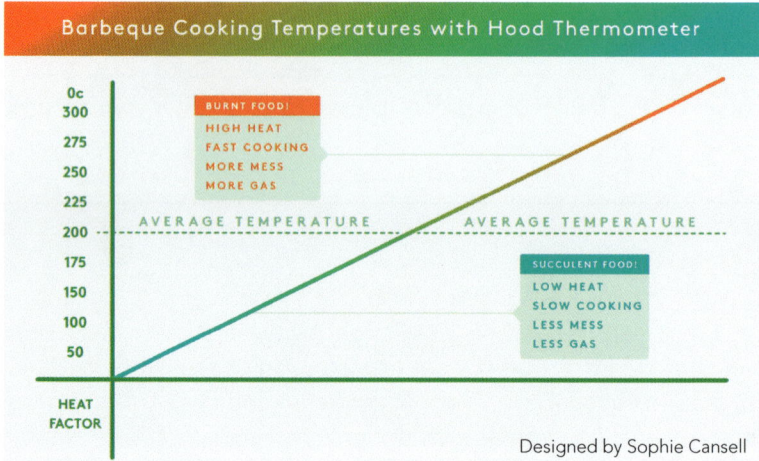

Designed by Sophie Cansell

PREPARATION

Almost every Chef and Cook out there will tell you 'Preparation' is the heart of many a good BBQ. If your Preparation is done, your cooking will be so much easier:

Make sure that the BBQ is ready:

Have you got enough gas?

Is the charcoal lit up and ready to go?

Is the meat out of the freezer and at room temperature?

Are the Veggies washed, diced, sliced and ready?

Is the BBQ clean and preheated?

Have you got oil for marinating?

Spatulas, tongs, and plates ready?

Make sure there is no cross-contamination.

As we said earlier, check your guests for fads and allergies before they arrive.

Meat thermometers ready?

There are more but if you make a list each time you BBQ, these reminders will come as naturally as cooking on it!

More hints and tips can be found on each of the author's websites:

www.bbqben.com & www.barbitec.com

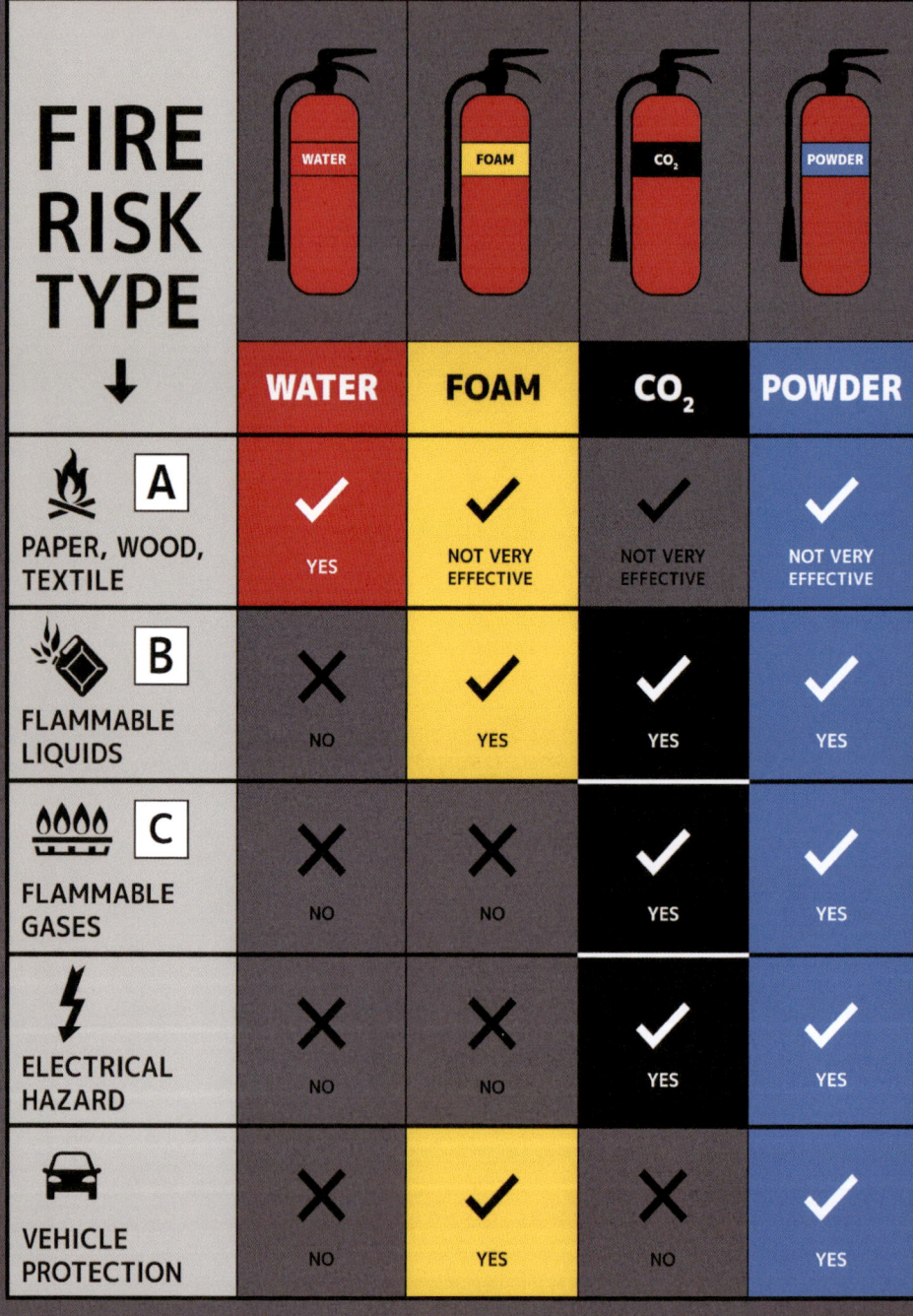

BBQ SAFETY

Like any appliance, whether Gas or Charcoal, there are some risks involved in using a BBQ.

Firstly, a BBQ should never be used inside*, whether a Gas or charcoal BBQ, some toxic gases are given off, such as carbon monoxide, which is odourless and colourless and, as such, is called the 'silent killer'.

However, it is perfectly safe to use either in an outdoor situation, electric, gas, coal, or wood; all these are perfectly safe.

Remember that Barbecues get very hot, so make sure that children are kept away from the BBQ when you are cooking, and never leave a BBQ completely unattended. Many a fire has been caused by leaving a BBQ alone, and as the BBQ cook, you need to keep an eye on the cooking. If you do need to go into the kitchen to get something, just turn the burners down or close the vents for a charcoal BBQ while you are away; that way the BBQ will just simmer for a bit until you get back to it.

It may sound silly but get your Gas BBQ serviced every two years; any qualified gas person can service it, but NOT a handyman!

People ask me, 'Why would you get a BBQ serviced?' Well, I have run a business for over 20 years just doing that, servicing gas BBQs!

Now, Gas bottles - In Australia, we use propane; in the UK, they use a combination of Propane and Butane, some just butane. Certain BBQs can use both, but you will need to check on the BBQ to ascertain which one can be used.

If you do, unfortunately, have a fat fire on either a charcoal or Gas BBQ that gets out of control, the best thing to do is use a dry powder extinguisher (if you have one) and, if that is not available, a fire blanket to smother the flames. DO NOT lift it up and down. Just smother it and leave it. A damp towel is also very effective.

**BUT ALWAYS, IF YOU THINK THE FIRE WILL BE A THREAT TO LIFE OR HOME CALL THE FIRE BRIGADE! **

British & Australian BBQ Secrets

Now, that's just a few pieces of advice from Ben and myself, just be conscious of your BBQ, be there when you light it or fire it up, check the connections and the heat, make sure it doesn't overheat and continually check the food you put on it.

Last tip! Don't overcook, you can always go forward if something is not cooked, but you can never go back if it's overcooked!

*Some BBQs are approved for indoor use but have safety devices to ensure safe use

CLEANING UP!

This is the part that we BBQ Chefs and would-be cooks always like, isn't it? The end of the lovely BBQ and the clearing and cleaning…!

But this doesn't have to be a chore; yes, some people get professional cleaners to clean their BBQ up so it looks like new, but others have or like to clean it themselves.

Now these below are great tips for keeping your BBQ sparkling and ready to go.

18. DO NOT use lots of oil and fat on your BBQ; not only does it make the food greasy, but it is also a fat fire risk.

19. Always check the drip tray to make sure that the leftovers from last time, fat and food aren't sitting in the tray; not only does it look and smell awful, but it also attracts pests, vermin and in OZ cockroaches, Yuk! Clean and use foil and change after each BBQ.

20. Your food will always need resting, so make this the time to clean your BBQ. Scrape any leftovers off the plate and grill, wipe with a damp cloth and dry with a paper towel, then use a canola oil spray to lubricate the plates and grills.

21. <u>BIG TIP</u>**!!!**

 DO NOT UNDER ANY CIRCUMSTANCES USE A BUCKET OF WATER OR GARDEN HOSE ON YOUR BBQ!

 Not only does it make a mess, but it also can damage the electrics on a gas BBQ and spread the ash all over the place on a charcoal one.

22. <u>Maintain the burners</u>. Make sure that the burners (gas BBQ) are clean and the ports (little holes where the gas flame comes out) are clear and not blocked. If they are blocked, this will affect the performance and the heat.

23. Some Barbecues are easy to clean, some a lot harder, but the majority of manufacturers make it easy to take the burners out. Again, do not soak any burners in water; point the hose at them or put them in the dishwasher.! **Yes, some say that it's ok, but trust us, it's not!**

British & Australian BBQ Secrets

24. When you decide to clean your BBQ, have the following handy and use them:

A damp soapy sponge

A scraper

Some paper towels

A bucket of water

An area in your garden that doesn't matter if it gets dirty!

Take the grills and plates out, then the burners if you can, scrub the plates / grills and clean the inside of the BBQ, dry with paper towels and put back the plates etc.

When using a cleaner, try and avoid market brands of cleaners; they are expensive, mostly caustic and after a while, will damage your BBQ; natural cleaning products are the best or soapy water on a damp sponge or cloth is usually best.

As we explained before, try not to leave cleaning your BBQ for too long; after every second BBQ is normal for a good clean. As if it's left for too long, the fat and grease builds up, and it makes it harder to get it back to where it was.

25. Always try and clean when the BBQ is still warm, the oils and fat are still runny, your food is resting, and the wine, beer and drinks are flowing. However, It only takes about 5 minutes to make the BBQ bearable for the next cookout, and your guests won't even miss you!

Using less oil when you cook, and leaner quality meats will make it easier to clean and much quicker.

Obviously, if you have just used a heavy marinade, it will take longer to clean, but 5 minutes will get the worst off, and you can give it a better clean the next day.

26. Now, Charcoal Barbecues are a little bit different and very easy to clean, so take the charcoal dust out, wipe the frame with a wet cloth, clean the grills and there you go.

27. You need to Keep your investment looking great (yes there are BBQs out there over $10,000 or £5000 or more, and in my own experience (Ross speaking here), they rarely get looked after; it's almost 'out of sight – out of mind', cleaning is all part of cooking.

British & Australian BBQ Secrets

'For instance, in a commercial kitchen, cleaning is part of the hospitality culture, so you should make cleaning your BBQ part of the culture too.

Once you get into a routine, it's easy and fun, yes fun to clean up as you are getting ready for the next BBQ, same as a kitchen gets ready for the next service; it all goes hand in hand.

Barbecuing is a great way to learn to cook. Yes, you make mistakes, Ben & Ross make mistakes, and you will too, but that is all part of the learning process; how do you think they learnt?

This will be the first of a series of books; this one is volume one, and the next will be a little harder. Once you have the technique, the BBQ gets easier to cook on, maybe Fish, Gourmet, Asian, African, Mexican, or South American; it's all doable.

Anyway, we digress a bit, back to basic cleaning…

Just remember not to use any oil on the plates and grills other than spray oil (canola is the best as it has a high smoke point and won't burn) Extra Virgin Olive oil has a low smoke point, so it's best to brush EVOO on the food rather than on the BBQ as otherwise as soon as it hits the BBQ plate it will burn. EVOO burns at about 180c and Canola oil at about 220c. This is called the 'Smoke Point'.

Well, that's it for this chapter a few basic hints and tips, just try them and let Ross & Ben know if you have any other tips that you may use that they haven't thought of.

Their websites are at the front of the book as well as their mobile numbers. Just remember the time difference between the **UK & OZ,** so maybe best to leave a message if they don't pick up.

Remember that they are both busy BBQ Chefs, but they will try and get back to you as soon as they can…

Recipes

BBQ BUTTERFLIED LAMB 59

THE BEST BBQ RUMP STEAK 61

FANTASTIC HOT DOGS WITH ONION AND
DIJON MAYONNAISE 63

BBQ BACON SUSHI ROLL 67

GRILLED BBQ CHICKEN BURGERS 69

PORK & LEMONGRASS SKEWERS 71

"KORMA-STYLE" BBQ KEBABS 73

SKINNY PINEAPPLE & SHREDDED CHICKEN
SALAD WRAPS 77

ROSS'S BBQ MEATBALLS 81

BBQ PRAWNS 85

BBQ FISH CAKES / FISH BITES 87

CEDAR WOOD MACKEREL 91

VEGGIE BBQ KEBABS 93

WATERMELON PIZZA (V) 94

JACKET POTATOES IN FOIL 97

GRILLED ASPARAGUS RAFTS 99

COWBOY BEANS 101

CORN ON THE COB 103

BBQ CARAMELISED FRUIT WITH HONEYED
CREAM AND 'STICKY' SEMILLON 105

FLAMED BANANAS 109

Recipes from Ben & Ross
BBQ Butterflied Lamb

You will need 'Butterfly leg of Lamb' - make sure that it has nothing added to it like a marinade etc., just plain lamb.

Put your BBQ grill on too high, and hood up.

Now, if you get one that is quite thick cut it down the middle, so it is in two parts, the thick and the thin (We are going to use the thick part). If there is skin on one side, score it diagonally with a sharp knife but try not to cut into the meat; repeat in the other direction so you have a diagonal Criss cross effect.

Place it on a plate and brush both sides with a good extra virgin olive oil, then sprinkle a little cracked pepper and sea salt and some chopped rosemary. Next, heat a pan on the BBQ side burner or your kitchen hotplate if there is no side burner. After a couple of minutes, place the lamb in the pan and add a glug of red wine; after about 30 seconds, turn the lamb over and cook the other side for another 30 seconds. The lamb should be starting to become crisp and charred on the outside.

Next, place it onto the grill in the middle, and turn the heat down to medium...OK, it will take about 10 to 20 minutes with occasional turning, depending on how you like it. The one in the picture was on for about 20/25 minutes, then take it off, cover it with foil and rest for at least 10 minutes; it should be lovely and moist with some juices to pour over when served.

The Best BBQ Rump Steak

Serves 8

Ingredients:

8 thick rump steaks (225g/8oz each cut to an even thickness)

4 tablespoons brown sugar

4 tablespoons sweet paprika

4 teaspoons dry mustard

4 teaspoons ground allspice

Pinch pepper

20mls BBQ Ben's Original BBQ sauce

Method:

- Combine the first five spice ingredients in a small bowl.
- Prepare the barbecue on a high heat.
- Rub the spice mixture generously on both sides of the steak.
- Grill the steak to your liking.
- Brush liberally with warmed BBQ sauce.

Fantastic Hot Dogs with Onion and Dijon Mayonnaise

These are cooked the same way as you would cook chipolatas...I remember one of the first times I cooked these on the BBQ; we had some friends over from England, and when we mentioned Hot Dogs, they thought of greasy sausages on the BBQ or soggy frankfurters...not this way!

Firstly, get some sausages, try not to get BBQ sausages as you really don't know what's in them, get some beef or pork sausages from your local butcher or supermarket, then some red onions (you can use ordinary, but the flavour is better in red). Some hot dog rolls, as soft as possible, some tomato Ketchup, Dijon Mustard, and Mayonnaise.

For 6 people

Ingredients:

6 sausages

6 hot dog rolls

2 red onions

A little Extra Virgin Olive Oil

3 heaped teaspoons of Dijon Mustard

3 heaped tablespoons Mayonnaise

A little Tomato Ketchup

Salt and pepper (to taste)

Method:

- Make up the Mayonnaise mix by mixing the Dijon and Mayonnaise in a small bowl.

- Then put the sausages over the plate on the warming rack, then put one burner on under the grill on high and with the hood down, leave for about 15 to 20 minutes; they should be ready by then.

- Meanwhile, cut each roll down the middle on one side only, not all the way through, so that one side is still attached quite firmly. Next, peel and slice the onions thinly so that they can cook quickly. Put the rolls and onions on one side.

- Check on the sausages; they should be almost done by now; if not, turn them over. Now leave the hood up and turn all the burners on under the plate and grill on to high; place the rolls "outside down" onto the grill at the rear of the BBQ, watch them carefully as you don't want to burn them, it will only take a few minutes to brown, then turn them over to do the inside (be careful not to split them in two). When they are ready, put them onto large or individual plates, cut side up and squeeze a little Tomato Ketchup into each roll.

- Next, turn the burners off under the grill and toss the onions in a bowl with about two tablespoons of Extra Virgin Olive Oil, then take the sausages off the rack, if you haven't already done so, and place them each into a roll.

- Toss the onions onto the hot plate with tongs for only a few minutes until cooked; again, the idea is to sear and seal them so that they are still crunchy when eaten, not soggy. When ready, turn off all the burners and put a few onions on each hot dog roll, finish with a large blob of Dijon mayonnaise and serve immediately. Believe me; your friends will not believe how scrumptious these are!

- Tip: if you find the mayonnaise mix is a bit thick, add a little lemon juice to thin it down a bit.

BBQ Bacon Sushi Roll

Serves 8

Ingredients:

12 Slices Dry Cured Back Bacon

500g Minced Beef

BBQ Ben's Original BBQ Sauce

50g BBQ Rub

50g Creamy Lancashire Cheese

25g Kettle Chips

Method:

› Line six slices of bacon in rows together onto a Sushi mat.

› In a bowl, combine the minced beef and rub together.

› Evenly distribute the mixture onto the bacon thinly.

› Place a line of cheese onto one end.

› Pressing firmly, roll the sushi mat up and un-roll again.

› Place on the grill for approx. Twenty minutes are occasionally turning on medium heat until cooked.

› Brush the roll during the final minutes of cooking with warmed BBQ Sauce.

› Roll in the crumbed kettle chips.

› Slice into portions and serve with extra BBQ Sauce.

Grilled BBQ Chicken Burgers

Ingredients:

4 chicken thighs, skin off

1 tbsp extra virgin olive oil

British & Australian BBQ Secrets

4 burger buns

1 garlic clove, crushed

4 tbsp mayonnaise

Juice of ½ lemon

2 tsp Dijon mustard (wholegrain or original)

Paprika

Salt & pepper

Method:

> Put the burners under the grill onto the highest setting and leave the barbeque to warm up for a few minutes.

> Mix the oil, garlic, and mayonnaise together in a small bowl. Add the mustard and the lemon juice and mix thoroughly. Add salt and pepper to taste.

> Using a pastry brush, dip into the mixture and lightly coat both sides of the chicken thighs.

> The grill should now be ready for cooking. Slice the buns in half and place them on the grill but keep a close eye on them as they won't take long to brown! Turn them over to brown both sides, then place the bottom half of each bun on your serving plate and brush with a little of the mayonnaise mix.

> Turn the burners under the grill down to low. Place the chicken thighs smooth side up onto the grill and leave them to cook for 4–5 minutes. Then turn them over and cook for a further 5 minutes or until cooked through. If they fl are up, move them to the front of the barbeque where it's cooler. When the chicken is ready, place them smooth side up on the bun and put a dollop of the mayonnaise mix on top. Finish with a sprinkle of paprika. Place the bun lids on the side of the chicken thighs at a 45 degree angle, so that half of the thigh is visible. This is to prevent the top of the buns getting soggy, and it also looks great! Serve with a green salad.

> Tip: You can roast some veggies at the same time as the chicken (if you have room on the hotplate), then when everything is ready pile the veggies on the plate first, then put the chicken on top and spoon the juices over. It tastes sumptuous and looks great!

Pork & Lemongrass Skewers

Serves 4

Ingredients:

300g lean minced pork

10g mint, finely chopped

10g chives, finely chopped

4 garlic cloves, finely chopped

10g granulated sugar

10ml soy sauce

1 lemon, freshly squeezed

8 lemongrass stalks approx. 9cm in length

Sea salt and black pepper

Method:

› Place the minced pork, garlic, mint, chives, soy sauce, sugar and lemon in a large bowl, season with salt and pepper and mix well.

› Divide into eight portions and mould each one into a ball around the lemongrass stalk.

› Grill the pork and lemon skewer for 6-8 minutes on each side until golden and cooked.

› Serve with warm pitta bread and cumin-curried yoghurt dip.

British & Australian BBQ Secrets

"Korma-Style" BBQ Kebabs

These are great as filler, a snack or even as a main course with rice; they have quite intense flavours and are quite different for the average BBQ party. Try them; you won't be disappointed!

Ingredients:

500g lamb mince

500g Beef mince

2 white onions – chopped finely

1 red onion – chopped finely

3 cloves garlic – crushed

1 tsp nutmeg

1 tsp cinnamon

1 large handful of fresh chopped parsley

1 tbsp red wine

1 tsp rock salt

1 tsp freshly ground pepper

20 kebab sticks

2 tbsp EVOO (Extra Virgin Olive Oil)

Method:

› Really easy this, put all the ingredients in a food mixer and mix until fairly fine; about 20/30 secs on high should do; make sure you scrape the sides so that it is all blended evenly. Take the mix out and, with your hands, form sausages about 20mm thick and about 100mm long, or whatever size you want to make them! Now either place them onto a serving plate (as they are) ready to cook or feed them onto kebab sticks, then place them on the serving plate.

› Brush over the EVOO so that they are all coated. Turn the burners on to high on your plate with the hood open for about 5-10 mins, then place the kebabs on the plate with the stick end towards you. Turn a few times till cooked, about 15-20 mins, and serve with dips: sweet chilli sauce with sour cream, Greek yoghurt, or tomato sauce etc.

› Note: you can also cook them with the hood down on a silicone paper-lined baking tray on the plate. Turn the grill burners on high with the hood down until temp reaches 190-200c. Lift the hood, place the tray on the hot plate and close the lid; turn the burners down to low, but watch the temp; if it drops, turn them up to high again. Cook for about 20 mins turning once or until cooked.

Skinny Pineapple & Shredded Chicken Salad Wraps

Serves 8

Ingredients:

500g chicken breast

250g fresh crushed pineapple

50mls BBQ Ben's Original BBQ Sauce

30mls non-fat Greek Yoghurt

2 stalks celery, diced

1 carrot, grated

1 red onion, thinly sliced

20g almonds, sliced

½ tsp salt

½ tsp black pepper

Cos lettuce leaves

8 Tortilla Wraps

Method:

› Grill the chicken breast for 15 minutes, turning once.

› Spray occasionally with apple juice.

- ❯ During the final minutes of cooking, baste with warmed BBQ sauce.
- ❯ Shred the chicken using two forks and placed it in a bowl.
- ❯ Add the remaining ingredients and evenly combine.
- ❯ Fill each wrap with lettuce leaves and the chicken salad mixture.

Ross's BBQ Meatballs

Ingredients:

500 g lean beef mince

1 ½ cups fresh breadcrumbs

½ red onion, finely chopped

1 garlic clove, crushed

1 egg beaten

1 tbsp fresh basil, chopped (or 1 tsp dried)

1 tbsp fresh oregano, chopped (or

1 tsp dried)

½ red capsicum, finely chopped

1 tsp paprika

½ tsp salt and 1tsp cracked pepper

Feeds 4 people or at a party as nibbles

10 mins to prepare, 20–30 mins to cook. A Hood is required.

Method:

> These are great as a nibble with your sauce of choice, such as tomato, BBQ, or sweet chilli sauce and sour cream. They also taste great as part of a pasta sauce!

> Thoroughly mix all ingredients (except the breadcrumbs and egg) in a glass bowl, then add the egg and about half the breadcrumbs. Mix again and then add the rest of the breadcrumbs. You should end up with a fairly firm mix.

- To make the meatballs, take a spoonful of the mixture and roll it up into a 1-inch diameter ball. Repeat until all the mixture is used up. Place the meatballs on greaseproof paper on a tray and covered with cling wrap.

- Refrigerate for a minimum of one hour. This will make them a lot firmer which is better for cooking.

- Light two burners under the grill and pre-heat on high, with the hood closed, Until the temperature reaches 200–220°C. Spray the meatballs all over with A little canola oil and place the balls in the warming rack over the grill.

- Close the hood and turn the burners down to medium and cook for about 10 minutes. Then turn them over and cook with the hood down for a further 10 minutes. They should be done by now, but allow a little longer if they're not cooked through. The temperature will drop a bit, but this is normal, and it's better to cook them slowly than to burn them!

- Serve immediately on their own or with a yoghurt dip (Greek style yoghurt is the best as it's a bit thicker) or any of the above suggestions.

BBQ Prawns

BBQ prawns are easy to cook and are a typical Aussie dish for the barbeque. However, many people overcook them, and they become rubbery and tasteless! Cook prawns quickly for a juicy, tender result.

You can buy prawns raw or already cooked. There are many different varieties available, including banana prawns, tiger prawns and endeavour prawns. However, the king prawn is the most popular for cooking on the barbeque, as they are big and meaty and easy to handle with BBQ tongs. King prawns do come in different sizes and grades, but standard sizes are available in fish shops and supermarkets. Prawns can be bought frozen or fresh, but if you buy them frozen, remember that you can't refreeze them once they've thawed.

If you don't want the mess and hassle of peeling the prawns yourself, you can buy them already peeled. They are more expensive this way, but sometimes the extra cost justifies the effort of doing it yourself, especially if you need them ready in a hurry!

Prawn peelers, which de-vein and peel the prawns for you, are inexpensive and are available from kitchenware shops and department stores. Use the hotplate for cooking prawns – once heated, it cooks the prawns quickly and they retain their moisture better. It takes about 5 mins to prep about 10 - 20 prawns.

To cook BBQ prawns (Cooking time includes preheating BBQ hotplate), simply heat the hotplate for a few minutes on high, then turn the burners down to low heat and throw the prawns on. Cook them for 60–90 seconds (or 20 seconds if they've been pre-cooked), turning them two or three times, and then take them off the heat and serve immediately with lemon wedges. That's it!

BBQ Fish Cakes / Fish bites

Ingredients:

250-300 g good quality fish such as Barramundi cooked and flaked

1.5 tsp good quality Mayonnaise

2 heaped tsp fresh chopped parsley

½ to ¾ cup breadcrumbs

1 x egg

½ tsp sea salt

½ tsp cracked black pepper

Juice ½ lemon

1 tsp white wine vinegar

Seasoned flour

Canola Oil

Extra virgin Olive oil

Method:

› This is almost back to how Mum used to make fish cakes when I was young with a few extra bits thrown in. You can make cakes or fish bites.

› Put the BBQ Grill on to medium for about 3-5 minutes; place the fish fillet on some silicone paper and then a double wrap of foil, brush a little Olive Oil on the fish on both sides and then place the foiled fish onto the grill, turn the burners down to low and keep an eye on the fish so that it's not overcooked.

British & Australian BBQ Secrets

It will take about 3-5 minutes to cook before turning over, depending on the thickness.

› To check if ready, get a sharp knife and if it easily goes through the fish, it's ready; if you feel any resistance, it's not! Take it off the grill, then let it cool slightly, and gently flake it into a bowl, then add the mayo, lemon juice, parsley, egg, salt & pepper. Mix very gently until combined, then add the white wine vinegar.

› You should have a mushy combination. Add ½ of the breadcrumbs and mix, then the other half. It should now turn nice and firm ready to make into fish cakes or bites.

› Take about a palm full, ½ a cup and mould it into a fish cake (like a burger) and place it onto some grease proof paper or take about a tablespoon full and make it into a ball. Lightly coat each one in seasoned flour. Keep going till all the mixture is used.

› Then make sure your BBQ hotplate is clean and put it on too high for 5 minutes with the hood (if fitted) up. Place two tbsp canola oil mixed with 1 tsp olive oil onto the plate and watch just till it starts to smoke, then turn down to low. Put the fish cakes / bites onto the plate and cook for about 3-5 mins, then turn. Lift them up now and again to make sure they are not burning. If the plate is too cool, turn the heat up but be careful as the cakes are easy to burn.

› When ready, take off and place on some paper towels, and you are ready to eat. The cakes and bites can be dipped in tartar sauce / sweet chilli sauce/ ketchup / yoghurt etc.

›

Cedar Wood Mackerel

Serves 8

Ingredients:

1 tsp grated lime rind

50mls lime juice

1 Tbsp. rapeseed oil

1 tsp Wholegrain mustard

Pinch pepper

8 x 100g Mackerel fillets

Method:

> In a zip-lock bag, mix the rind, juice, oil, mustard, and pepper.
> Add the fish and coat well.
> Marinate for 10 minutes.
> Put the mackerel onto a cedar wood sheet that has been previously soaked in water for 10 minutes.
> Place the sheet onto the grill on low-medium heat.
> Grill for 10 minutes and serve.

Veggie BBQ Kebabs

Vegetable kebabs are ready for the BBQ, so easy get the BBQ grill on high for about 5 to 10 minutes with the hood up, then turn it to low. Drizzle the kebabs with EVOO and spices of your choice; I used Harissa. Cook until charred, turning regularly and serve...

Veggie kebabs, mushrooms, peppers (mixed colours), red onion, tomatoes, simple, colourful, effective and delicious!

Watermelon Pizza (V)

Serves 8

Ingredients:

1 whole Watermelon

4 Red Onions

100mls Red Wine Vinegar

20g Demerara Sugar

20g Sea Salt

300g Shropshire Blue Cheese

Bunch Basil leaves

British & Australian BBQ Secrets

Method:

> Peel and slice the onions into rings and put in a bowl.

> Add the red wine vinegar, sugar and salt and mix with a spoon. Leave to marinade for 10 minutes.

> Slice the watermelon into ½" slices.

> Place the onions onto the watermelon slices.

> Top with grated Shropshire blue cheese and chopped basil.

> Place on the grill and cook for 8-10 minutes until the cheese melts. Cut into wedges and serve at once.

Jacket Potatoes in Foil

This recipe is as easy as pie and very difficult to get wrong.

Take each potato and lightly scrub it in water and then pat it dry with a T towel or a paper towel.

Take a sharp knife and cut two slits into the potato halfway and two cuts the other way (like noughts and crosses) then place in foil about 6-7 inches square depending on the size of the spud. This helps them cook more quicker.

Drizzle with a little olive oil about half a teaspoon of butter and a few chopped fresh herbs (you can use mixed dry herbs if it's easier). Then lift each corner of the foil up to the top of the spud and give it a slight twist. Not too tight, or it won't be able to breathe.

Place on the warming rack of the BBQ and close the lid. Put the right-hand burner only on full if 4 burner or less or two far-right burners on if 5 burners or more. The hood temp gauge should reach about 200c or a little less.

Leave for about 45 mins to 1 hour until cooked through. Don't worry if it takes longer and uses a sharp knife to poke through the foil to test. It should go easily through if ready.

The reason why I foil them this way is that they are easier to handle as you can grab them by the tops of the foil when ready, they don't stick to the foil, and they present better as you can serve them this way.

Serve with some sour cream so guests can help themselves if they wish.

Grilled Asparagus Rafts

Serves 4

Ingredients:

16 fresh asparagus spears

1 tbsp. low-sodium soy sauce

1 tsp dark sesame oil

1 garlic clove, finely chopped

2 tsp sesame seeds, toasted

Method:

- Cut off the tough ends off the asparagus.
- Thread two wooden skewers horizontally through four spears about one inch from each end.
- Continue with all the spears.
- In a bowl mix together the soy sauce, oil, and garlic.
- Brush over the asparagus.
- On a high heat grill for 3 minutes on each side and sprinkle with the sesame seeds.

Cowboy Beans

Serves 8

Ingredients:

4 tins of mixed beans

4 slices diced bacon

50g chopped onion

1 Tbsp. BBQ rub

300mls BBQ Ben's Original BBQ sauce

50g brown sugar

Method:

> Use a barbecue skillet to fry the bacon until crispy, add the onion and cook until soft.

> Transfer the bacon to a saucepan and add the onion, beans, rub, sauce, and brown sugar. Simmer for 15 minutes and serve.

Corn on the Cob

Serves 8

Ingredients:

8 corns on the cob

6 Tbsp. soft butter

1 Tbsp. chopped coriander

¼ tsp chilli powder

½ tsp ground cumin

Method:

- Combine the butter, coriander, chilli powder and cumin.
- Rub the ears of corn evenly with the mixture.
- Preheat the grill to medium-high and grill the corn for 15 minutes, turning occasionally.

BBQ Caramelised Fruit with Honeyed cream and 'sticky' Semillon

Ingredients:

1 tin sliced Peaches

1 tin pineapple pieces or rings

Some fresh strawberries (if in season)

Frozen mixed berries (half a cup)

2 tbsp Soft Brown Sugar

Big squeeze of fresh lime

Two Rivers 'Sticky' Semillon

Teflon sheet (Optional)

Note: the fruit above can be varied, such as Blueberries, raspberries, kiwi fruit, apricots – and you can use fresh or tinned

250ml whipped cream

2 x tbsp honey

1 tsp cinnamon

Method...

> Heat the BBQ plate on high for a minute or two then turn it down to medium; if it's dirty, make sure you give it a good clean and rub it with have of the lime. If you can buy Teflon

sheet and put that on the plate, it makes it very easy to clean afterwards!

› Ok, now cut up your fruit into pieces, not too small, discard all the juice if out of a can and place in a bowl, add the mixed berries (about half a cup). Meanwhile (and this can be done earlier), place 250ml of the semi-firm cream in another bowl, add the honey, mix gently, then add the cinnamon.

› Now, this bit is very important and needs to be done quickly; put the whole lot directly onto the plate, add about ¼ cup of the Semillon till it starts to bubble, then add the sugar and toss lightly for a minute, then lastly, add the squeeze of lime once it's heated scoop it off being careful not to tear the sheet (if used) and place onto a plate or individual plates.

› Don't let it stay on the plate longer than about two minutes, or it will burn or stew.

› Add a large dollop of the honeyed cream and a sprinkle of the cinnamon for effect, and there you have BBQ caramelised fruit with honeyed cream and sticky Semillon.

Flamed Bananas

Serves 4

Ingredients:

4 bananas, slightly under-ripe

150mls double cream

4 vanilla pods, split and deseeded

40g butter

40g sugar

100mls brandy

Method:

> Whisk the cream, 10g sugar and half the vanilla pod seeds in a bowl and place in the fridge.

> Warm the butter, remaining sugar and vanilla in a pan, split the bananas down the back and pour over the mixture.

> Wrap the bananas individually in foil and place on the barbecue for 8-10 minutes until warmed.

> Meanwhile, gently warm the brandy in a small pan. Open each banana parcel and pour over the brandy. Carefully ignite with a long match, watch, and enjoy!

Glossary

If you want to hang with the professionals, here are some more unusual BBQ terms:

ABT

An acronym for "Atomic Buffalo Turd" and made by slicing a hot pepper in half, filling it with cream cheese and BBQing it until soft.

Arvo

Australian for afternoon, 'have a BBQ in the arvo'.

Bark

The firmer flavour-bursting surface layer of crust forms on a brisket.

Bend Test

A simple test for checking if smoked ribs are done. Pick up the rack, and if they are ready, the ribs will bow until the meat starts to break away.

Brine

A solution of water, salt and sometimes sugar and various herbs soaked into cheaper cuts of meat to improve the flavour and texture.

Bring a plate

Not just bring a plain plate but bring some food on a plate to share.

Burnt Ends

These crispy, fatty squares of smoked brisket are also known as "meat candy" in the USA.

Chook

Aussies word for Chicken.

Chuck

Known as bolar blade beef in Australia and is used a lot there for a roast as it doesn't dry out as much.

Cold Smoking

Cheese, spices, and many fish are good when cold-smoked at a temperature between 90F/32C and 120F/50C.

Cowboy Barbecue

BBQing rustically above an open bed of charcoal.

Creosote

Unhealthy sticky, bitter, black components consolidate on cool surfaces of meat and your BBQ when wood is wrongly burned.

Dry Rub

A combination of herbs and spices rubbed into food prior to grilling.

Esky

A cool box to take your beer and wine in.

Firebox

Usually, a part of a smoker cooker is to the side that the charcoal rests in.

Footprint

How much space a BBQ takes up on your patio. An important consideration when purchasing a BBQ and keeping 'the Mrs.' happy.

Grill Basket

A metal pan with holes to contain small food items on the BBQ and not slip between the grills.

Grog

Australian term for Alcohol.

Indirect Cooking

Food is placed at the side of the fuel source instead of directly over the heat.

Injection

Literally injecting a larger joint of meat before cooking with marinade to infuse the meat with extra flavour.

Jerk

This type of cooking is instinctive in Jamaica, where meats and fish are rubbed with a hot spicy mixture.

Kamado

These ceramic cookers originated in Japan and can grill or smoke foods.

Liquid Smoke

This is produced by smoke passed through water and is used for food preservation and flavouring.

Low 'n' Slow

BBQing on low heat under 275F/135C over time, resulting in the fats and collagens breaking down and making meat moist and full of flavour.

Lump Charcoal

Made from real wood pieces that light fast, burn hot and leave less ash than briquettes.

Money Muscle

This part of pork shoulder is moist and tasty and often wins the prize money at BBQ contests.

Mop

A mopping brush is used to apply a basting sauce on a piece of meat to add a burst of flavour and caramelisation.

Pitmaster

The King of the BBQ who controls the red-hot coals to create smoky, delicious morsels of perfection.

Plank Cooking

This is the technique of roasting fish and game on wood planks, wood sheets or papers for extra wood aroma and flavour.

Power Cook

The Process of cooking at a higher than normal temperature speeds up the cooking process.

Pork Butt

This tough cut of meat from the upper section of the shoulder is used to create delicious slow-cooked tender pulled pork.

Shiners

This is an over-butchered rack of ribs that shows exposed bones once cooked that "shine throughout" the meat.

Skin 'n' Trim

Preparing ribs by removing the membrane on the underside that can become tough when grilled and trimming any excess fat and loose flaps of meat.

Slider

A mini bite-sized burger.

Stubbie

What Aussies call a bottled beer.

Smoke Ring

A chemical reaction happens when smoking meat that can lead to a coveted pink hue called the "smoke ring" that appears just underneath the skin and is often considered the sign of a good brisket.

Teatime

This is called Dinner time in OZ; confusing sometimes.

Texas Crutch

This refers to the use of aluminium foil for wrapping meat during cooking BBQ.

Thermapen

A thermometer that shows internal food temperatures in seconds.

Tinnie

What Aussies call a can of beer.

Tongs

For handling food on the BBQ.

Tucker

Australian for food.

Turducken

Created by stuffing a de-boned dressed chicken and putting it into a de-boned dressed stuffed duck, which itself is put into a de-boned dressed stuffed turkey.

Yard-bird

Slang word for a chicken.

Printed in Great Britain
by Amazon